Care and Breeding of Popular Tree Frogs

Philippe de Vosjoli
Robert Mailloux
Drew Ready

The Herpetocultural Library

Advanced Vivarium Systems, Inc.

10728 Prospect Ave., Suite G, Santee, CA 92071

Library of Congress Cataloging-in-Publication Data- IN PROCESS

ISBN 1-882770-36-6

Printed in Korea
Represented by Codra Enterprises, Inc., in Carson, CA

Cover photography by David Northcoff

Contents

Introduction

S LOWLY, SOME WOULD say at a snail's pace, herpetoculture in the
United States is moving toward an environment-based
herpetoculture that focuses on the design of naturalistic vivaria: captive
environments that simulate some of the essential characteristics of the
natural habitats of amphibians and reptiles. This trend has led to an
increased interest in smaller animals that display well and can thrive
in these new kinds of vivaria. Among some of the best vivarium
animals are tree frogs, creatures that often anchor to glass sides or
perch on vivarium plants. Many of the tree frogs particularly the
smaller species, can be kept with other small frogs and small lizards in
a community vivarium, a combination which has great display appeal.
These factors have led to a growing interest in the herpetoculture of
these frogs. Unfortunately, just as the interest in tropical amphibians
is increasing, availability appears to be steadily diminishing, the result
of lack of knowledge, lack of standards for commercial exploitation,
protective legislation (some of which is very unsound), habitat destruction, and environmental and climatic changes. If humans are to enjoy
frogs and other amphibians in the future, immediate attention must be
given to sound conservation, research, and management of various
species. Our view is that establishing as many self-sustainable populations of as many species as possible in herpetoculture is imperative
because humans have much to gain from the experience of observing
frogs in captivity as well as from scientific research on frogs.

Our goal originally was to write a simple, basic book on the care
of popular tree frogs, but in the writing process it became obvious that
keeping frogs successfully requires certain skills and knowledge much
like keeping tropical fish: it's just not that simple. Although there are
now on the market a number of books about the care of amphibians,
several were written by authors with little or no experience in keeping

or breeding frogs. In spite of all the pretty pictures, such books contain little information of real value.

This book, written by experienced and recognized frog herpetoculturists, focuses on the care of popular tree frogs now sold in significant numbers in pet stores. It covers many important topics, from acclimating imported species to housing, feeding, and captive-breeding. It is a practical manual for the serious hobbyist who cares about the welfare of his or her animals.

General Information

What are Tree Frogs?

Tree frog is a popular term for nocturnal frogs that are arboreal to semiarboreal and have toe pads at the ends of their digits. Tree frog is the common name usually reserved for members of the family Hylidae, but the popular herpetocultural definition also includes the glass frogs (family Centronelidae), reed frogs (family Hyperolidae) and flying frogs (family Rhacophoridae).

Selecting Tree Frogs

If you are new to the keeping of tree frogs your best bet is to begin with easy-care species such as White's tree frogs *(Litoria caerulea)*, white-lipped tree frogs *(Litoria infrafrenata)*, green tree frogs *(Hyla cinerea)* or Cuban tree frogs *(Osteopilus septentrionalis)*. Other tree frogs require some experience, particularly if they are wild-caught imports. If you follow the instructions in this book, you should also have success with moderately difficult to-care-for species such as the popular red-eyed tree frogs.

As a rule, species requiring cool temperate conditions, cloud forest species, and tropical rainforest species tend to be more difficult to keep than the more adaptable temperate and subtropical species. This is usually because cool cloud-forest species and rainforest species can have specific habitat requirements—such as a particular landscape, temperature range, relative humidity range, or air flow—which need to be duplicated if they are to survive for a long time. Researching the habitat and niche of particular tree frogs, acquiring experience at establishing frogs, and setting up the right type of vivaria will, however, allow you to successfully keep and breed these more difficult species.

This book focuses on the care of the easy-to-keep and readily available species offered in the general pet trade, with the exception of

A healthy White's tree frog (Litoria caerulea) has very smooth rounded contours.

the gliding tree frogs. These have been included because of their appeal and the problems generally encountered at acclimating them to captivity.

The first step to keeping tree frogs successfully is to select the species that you can comfortably accomodate. The second step is to select potentially healthy animals.

Captive-bred versus wild-caught specimens

White's tree frogs are captive-bred in large numbers in the United States and are generally easy to rear to adulthood. Other captive-bred species are less frequently available and can be difficult to rear because of their small size or special requirements when they are young. Wild-caught adults of the popular species mentioned in this book (with the exception of gliding tree frogs) are relatively easy to establish in captivity and are probably as good a bet as captive-bred frogs. On the other hand, the more difficult species, whether wild-caught or captive-bred, will prove challenging and very possibly disappointing to the inexperienced herpetoculturist.

Selecting healthy tree frogs

A critical prerequisite if you want to have success with tree frogs is the selection of potentially healthy specimens. The following guidelines should significantly increase your chances of success.

1.   Select species that you think you are capable of accommodating. Do some research on their needs and their vivarium design requirements. Providing the proper conditions for a particular species of frog is critical to its establishment and survival in captivity.

2.   Observe the animals from which you will make your selection. As a rule, tree frogs that are up on the glass sides or the landscape structures of a vivarium will prove to be healthier than those that remain on the ground. This is a guideline, not a rule fixed in stone; tree frogs kept in the wrong kind of vivarium may be stressed and thus seek terrestrial shelters or lie on the ground to reduce dehydration or to seek cooler temperatures. Sometimes the problem is that the seller or the store owner does not provide the proper vivarium landscape.

3.   Carefully inspect the animal. It should not have sores, lumps, swollen legs, or clouded eyes. Its body should appear rounded, and the outlines of its hip bones and backbone should not be prominent. Neither should the outline of bones of the skull be prominent.

4.   When held in your hand, the frog you select should demonstrate definite signs of vigor. Frogs that feel limp and weak are usually very ill. Once you have a frog in hand, inspect its body more closely including its ventral area (underside), for sores or redness. Avoid animals that have these symptoms of illness.

5.   If the frogs for sale are kept with paper as a substrate, look for signs of feces. Watery, runny feces are usually a sign of illness. Bloody feces are definitely a sign of illness.

If the frog you are selecting has met most of the criteria for health previously mentioned, there is a good chance that it is relatively healthy and will acclimate if provided with the proper conditions.

Aerosols and Miticides
Aerosol sprays such as hair spray, perfume deodorants, and disinfectants such as Lysol®, can kill tree frogs. These aerosols can be asborbed through the skin. Do not keep frogs in areas such us bathrooms where aerosols are used. No Pest strips, used for killing mites will also kill frogs at high concentrations or over long-term exposure.

Acclimation

THE FOLLOWING STEPS will allow you to establish tree frogs that have been imported or caught in the wild.

1. Keep any newly acquired frog in a room with a cool-air humidifier (available at most drug stores), which will keep the relative humidity at 60 to 70 percent. Humidifiers are not necessary in regions with moderate to high relative humidity. Do not keep frogs at saturated humidity levels (above 85 percent).

2. To create a tree frog vivarium, place any new frog in a large plastic terrarium or glass vivarium with white paper towel as a substrate and a shallow water bowl or plant saucer as a source of water. With baby frogs add a shallow container filled with moist moss. Add a piece of

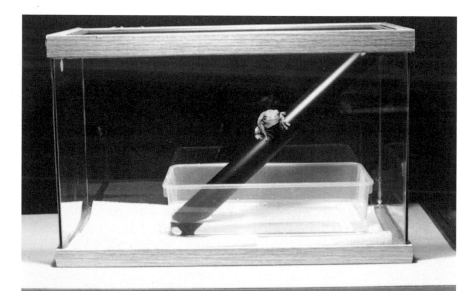

A basic vivarium for quarantine and temporary housing of tree frogs. Although many adult tree frogs can be kept long-term in this manner, this type of vivarium does not really provide the conditions for a good quality of life. Larger vivaria with plants and climbing areas are preferable even if the substrate remains newsprint.

For quarantining red-eyed tree frogs plants should be added to the enclosure either in pots or grown hydroponically in jars of water. Chinese evergreen (Aglaonema commutatum) and pothos are the best choices.

bark leaning against one side of the terrarium as a vertical shelter and another on the ground as a ground-level shelter. Keep your vivarium at the appropriate temperature range for the species you are keeping. Provide moderately bright light with overhead full-spectrum fluorescent bulbs for 12 hours per day.

3. If the frog appears weak, has sores on its snout or other parts of its body, or has clouded eyes, monitor it for a few days to see if it is improving. If not, you can treat it with injectable Baytril® (enrofloxacin) subcutaneously in the ventral area at a dosage of 10 mg/kg of body weight. Repeat the treatment every 48 hours for as long as 14 days.

4. Monitor the stools of your frog during its acclimation period. Healthy frogs have soft but formed stools. Watery and runny stools are signs of parasites or gastrointestinal disease.

5. Offer crickets of the appropriate size to your tree frog every two to three days, and monitor the status of its feces. If feces are runny, then treat the frog orally with Flagyl® (metronidazole)at 50 mg/kg body weight. Repeat in one week. Flagyl used twice, seven days apart, during treatment with Baytril® can be beneficial because of its antibiotic effects on anaerobic bacteria. If your tree frog has nematodes in its stools, then treat with Panacur® (fenbendazole) at 50 mg/kg and

Baby tree frogs are very prone to dehydration. Most species will do best in a gravel bed type of vivarium. For quarantine or simple set-ups, baby tree frogs should be set with an area of moistened green moss and with a shallow water container. To prevent the risk of drowning in the water container a rock or strands of pothos vine should be put in the water. Plants growing hydroponically in jars of water are also recommended.

repeat once or twice at seven-day intervals. To administer drugs or water orally, use a plastic wedge cut from a plastic deli cup, or yogurt container, and insert it gently between the frog's jaws. For larger species or specimens, an inverted spoon can be gently inserted between the jaws to keep the mouth open.

6. If a frog refuses to feed, you can open its mouth and insert a prekilled cricket of the appropriate size in its mouth. In most cases, treefogs when released will swallow the cricket. Emaciated frogs, if not feeding on their own, should be assist-fed as soon as possible.

7. If a newly imported frog is sick or dehydrated, give it water orally in addition to providing a water bowl. Keep the water bowl clean and replace the water several times each week and whenever it is fouled. Mist tree frogs lightly every evening.

8. Replace the paper towel used as substrate when fouled. Keep water clean. Feed frogs every two to three days and monitor them closely. Healthy frogs are active at night, feed regularly, have formed feces, and eventually put on weight. Transfer your frog to a larger vivarium as soon as it shows signs of acclimating to captivity. Warning: Quarantine your frog in a vivarium for at least 60 days before introducing it in a vivarium containing established animals.

Housing

Principles of Vivarium Design for Tree Frogs

1. Basic vivarium suitable for quarantine or maintenance

A basic vivarium for tree frogs should consist of an all-glass enclosure with a screen top. For most species a minimum size of 20 gallons is recommended. Tree frogs are active, and in the authors' opinion smaller enclosures do not provide the conditions for a good quality of life for them. You can use smaller vivaria for quarantine and for the rearing of tree froglets. In terms of density of animals, a good general rule for most adults of most species is: at least a 20-gallon vivarium and a frog-to-volume ratio of one animal per five gallons. With very large species such as White's tree frogs or White-lipped tree frogs, the authors recommend at least a 29-gallon vivarium with a minimum frog-to-volume ratio of one per 15 gallon's of vivarium space.

You can place sliding screen-top vivaria on their sides to create a vertical vivarium. Ideally you would use silicone to attach a section of acrylic or glass across the base, thereby making a bottom that will hold substrate or water without it seeping through or clogging the screen.

In a simply designed vivarium, newsprint or white paper towels can be used as a substrate during quarantine with many species, but it will not work with species requiring high relative humidity unless the frogs are kept in a room with a cool-air humidifier. An alternative with species that require high relative humidity is to use a $1^{1}/_{2}$- to 2-inch layer of smooth medium-grade pea gravel as a substrate. Make sure the pea gravel is large enough that your frogs cannot swallow it accidentally. If you add water up to half the substrate height, the surface of the substrate will remain dry, while the bottom will contain enough water to raise relative humidity. Provide water in a shallow container such as a dog's water bowl or a plastic storage box (shoe

Step-by-Step Naturalistic Vivarium Design

Step 1

Many tree frogs do well in a gravel bed vivaria. To create a gravel bed shallow shoreline vivarium, essentially simulating a water's edge, first add a 2-3 inch layer of washed pea gravel or larger grade aquarium gravel. In one corner push the gravel aside to create a water area and edge it with larger smooth stones to prevent gravel from sliding back in. Insert in the gravel plants that will grow well hydroponically. The plants should be rinsed free of soil. A hollow dug out in the gravel, the plant inserted and gravel gently placed around the roots to anchor the plants. The best choice with tree frogs is Chinese evergreen (Aglaonema). Other good plants are pothos (Epipremnum), arrowhead plants (Syngonium) and philodendron. Other plants such as bromeliads and calathea can be placed in pots on top of the gravel bed.

box size). The water level in the container should be no higher than that of the frogs at rest.

Landscaping a simple vivarium: Place live plants such as pothos ivy or Chinese evergreen in jars of water or in gravel and water. These will serve as resting sites and help raise the relative humidity in the vivarium. If the air temperature is cool, then you can use a red 25-watt (or-higher) incandescent light bulb over a basking site. Fluorescent full-spectrum lighting is recommended as a primary source of light, both for the frogs and for the plants. You can raise relative humidity by increasing the number of plants in jars.

Step 2

Cork bark and freshwater driftwood can be added for shelters and climbing areas. Then a layer of moistened green moss is placed above large sections of the gravel substrate. This system works well with most Hyla species such as green tree frogs (Hyla cinerea), gray tree frogs (Hyla versicolor), Pacific tree frogs (Hyla regilla), Chinese jade treefrogs (Hyla chinensis) and a wide range of tropical forest and rainforest treefrogs including red-eyed tree frogs (Agalychnis callidryas). Good ventilation is essential as well as above ground shelters and climbing areas. To maintain, pour water over the moss area once a week to flush out wastes, siphon or vacuum water (industrial wet and dry vacuum cleaner available in major hardware stores) once a week and replace with clean water added directly to the water area (NOT poured over the moss).

Water: Place a shallow water bowl in the container with clean water (see section on water).

The preceding system works as a simple system for maintaining a wide range of tree frog species.

2. Flush system using a pebble substrate

A flush system with a pebble substrate works best with large vivaria, at least 30 gallons and preferably larger.

In this type of enclosure, place a layer 2 to 4 inches thick of medium-grade smooth pea gravel on the bottom. At one end, push back the gravel to excavate a pool area, essentially exposing the glass bottom of the enclosure. You can add rock or freshwater driftwood on the surface of the gravel. Various plants that can grow hydroponically (see chart) can be planted as bare-root plants in the gravel bed. Additional plants can be placed in pots, with only part of the pot buried in the gravel.

Next, soak green sheet-moss in a bucket of water and then place it over the gravel, covering the base of the plants but leaving the edges of the pool and the pool itself clear of the moss. Place smooth round rocks along the edges of the pool to prevent gravel from sliding in, and for aesthetic purposes as well. Then add water to a depth of as much as 2 inches in the enclosure. The pool will fill up but the gravel surface will remain dry. You also can add a miniature waterfall to this system.

The advantage of gravel bed vivaria is in keeping animals and plant species that require high relative humidity. Maintenance consists of misting plants daily. Once a week, you must pour water over the substrate to flush wastes into the pool area. You can then remove the fouled water with a wet/dry vacuum cleaner. Wipe the bottom of the water section with paper towel to remove algae and slime that may have accumulated on the surface. Add fresh water to the water section, but not over the substrate. The plants growing hydroponically will help remove ammonia, as will algae growing on rocks and other surfaces. If the gravel layer is deep, then you can add soil over one section of the layer and introduce plants directly in the soil layer. You can make this system more effective by adding a small water pump that move's water from the water area through the gravel substrate, which then becomes a biological filtering system.

Healthy frogs experience minimal problems with this system. Weekly flushing prevents the buildup of bacteria from wastes in the system. You can conduct ammonia and nitrite tests to monitor the quality of the water. More complex flush systems can be designed, but these will be covered in a future book specializing in shoreline vivaria.

ORCHID BARK
Fir bark based orchid bark and NOT Cedar bark can be used with treefrogs. The bark should be kept dry. Orchid bark kept wet for prolonged periods of time may leach out compounds that may be harmful to treefrogs if absorbed.

Filtered flush systems: More elaborate versions of the flush system run the water in the water section through a filter. You can use one of two methods to create such a system. One is to move the water over the gravel substrate as indicated previously. The other is to pump the water through a box containing a filtering medium. Pool filters work well in large vivaria, but you can constructed simple box filters from food storage boxes, drilled and filled with carbon and filter floss or filter pads.

3. Naturalistic vivarium

The naturalistic vivarium is one of the most popular systems in Europe for keeping frogs. In a large enclosure, place a 1- to 2-inch layer of pea gravel on the bottom. Above that add a 2- or 3- inch layer of moistened high-quality peat moss-based potting soil. Plant various tropical plants directly in the growing medium. Plants that are appro priate include pothos ivy, Chinese evergreen, calatheas, philodendron, alocasia, and bromeliads that don't have spiny edges, such as neorogelias. In addition, add landscape structures such as rock or wood and cork. Bury a water container in the soil and add water to the container. Twice a week, remove the water container, wash it

Smaller tropical tree frogs and poison-dart frogs (Dendrobates) in gravel bed type vivaria are combinations that work well. Smaller tropical anoles can also be kept in this kind of set-up.

thoroughly, and replace the water. Disinfect the container in a 5 percent bleach solution once a month, then rinse it out and allow it to soak in water with a dechlorinator for at least an hour to remove all traces of chlorine before placing it back in the vivarium.

An alternative to using a water container is to use a water section with a filter. You can do this by attaching with aquarium silicone sealer a section of glass 2 to 3 inches tall to the sides and bottom of an all-glass vivarium to create a water section. A small water pump can run the water through a filter canister or through a sponge filter, which operates with an air pump. Another alternative is to use an undergravel filter cut to size. This will require adding a 1- to 2-inch layer of pea gravel on top of the filter plates. The draw back of fixed-water sections is that they need to be cleaned regularly and the water must be changed regularly or it will become a vector for disease. Filters also must be cleaned or replaced on a regular basis.

Heating and Cooling

Heating

Most tree frogs do not bask in sunlight like many reptiles, although several species appear to enjoy basking, usually in the later part of the day. Because of this basking lights are not a good way to heat tree frog enclosures. Because light and intense heat tend to be offensive to these crepuscular or nocturnal anurans, other methods of heating must be devised. In general, frogs should be kept within rooms that are in the range of their temperature tolerances. Room temperatures in the mid 70s are suitable for most tree frogs although certain montane and cool-climate species require colder temperatures. Once the temperature in the room is in the general range of your tree frogs' requirements, you can provide supplemental heat by using subtank heating pads, heating strips controlled by rheostat or thermostat, or submersible heaters within the water section that are adjusted to keep the water in the correct temperature range. Other methods used by herpetoculturists include placing submersible heaters in large jars of water and placing 25-watt red incandescent bulbs over select areas. Low-wattage infrared ceramic bulbs also work in large enclosures if they can be controlled by a a rheostat or pulse-proportional thermostat. In the authors' opinion, keeping frogs in rooms that are heated to their temperature range with no additional heating is the best course when keeping large numbers of frogs.

Cooling

Few tree frog species currently collected or imported for the pet trade require unusually cool temperatures. If you do decide to keep cool-temperature or montane species then you must cool a room by using an air conditioner on a thermostat. On a temporary basis or during a heat crisis, you can place jars of ice in a vivarium and cover it with styrofoam. In dry climates, "swamp coolers" may be adequate for bringing a room's temperature down to a satisfactory level.

Relative Humidity

Relative humidity is a critical factor for the successful maintenance and breeding of frogs. Most frogs thrive at a 60 to 70 percent moderate relative humidity. This level is easily maintained in naturalistic vivaria or vivaria with hydroponic plants. If necessary, the relative humidity of a room can be raised easily with a cool-air humidifier. Light mistings of a vivarium one or more times per day will also increase relative humidity. Saturated humidity levels with no ventilation are fatal to most tree frogs. Never keep tree frogs in *glass covered* vivaria. You can condition many tropical tree frogs for breeding by keeping them at a lower relative humidity for a few weeks or months, thereby simulating a dry season. During this conditioning, you perform no misting and you keep the frogs drier, leaving a water container as the primary source of moisture. Relative humidity can be measured with hygrometers.

Feeding

Diet

All tree frogs are primarily insectivorous, although large specimens occasionally ingest vertebrate prey. The easiest approach to feeding tree frogs is to offer them commercially raised insects.

The following are guidelines on the use of these insects.

Gray crickets *(Acheta domestica)*

Gray crickets should be a primary component of the diet of captive tree frogs. These crickets are now regularly offered by most stores that sell amphibians and reptiles. They come in a variety of sizes suitable for feeding a wide range of tree frogs, from newly metamorphosed froglets to the giant species. A good general rule for determining the right size cricket for your frogs is that the length of the cricket should be about the same as the head length of the tree frog. This rule works with other kinds of food items also, even mice. Before being offered to tree frogs, crickets should be housed in a small plastic terrarium and fed a high quality diet for 24 hours (see section on high-quality diet for prey animals).

Flies

Housefly maggots can be bought by mail order. You can keep them in jars or screened enclosures until they pupate and metamorphose. Houseflies provide a cheap way to feed large numbers of froglets and a good supplemental food for adult tree frogs. As a rule they are best used in greenhouse facilities to avoid the annoyance of having escaped flies in your home. If however you allow them to pupate in jars, you can move them by using a nylon stocking with the toe-end cut off as a tube to guide the flies from pupating jars into frog vivaria.

Fruit flies

With very small tree froglets, the large flightless fruit fly *Drosophila hydei* now offered through mail order can be a good supplemental dietary item. (See reptile and fish magazines for sources.) These flies are easily raised on standard fruit fly mix, which is available by mail order or through biological supply houses.

Mealworms and king mealworms

Mealworms *(Tenebrio molitor)* and king mealworms *(Zophobas)* should be offered to tree frogs only as part of a varied diet. "White" (just molted) mealworms are more easily digested and are preferable as a diet to chitinized ones. Larger tree frog species fare better than smaller species on diets that include mealworms, particularly king mealworms.

Wax worms *(Galleria mellonella)*

As with mealworms, the caterpillars of the wax moth are best offered as part of a varied diet, although the metamorphosed moths are relished by many tree frogs. Wax moths can sometimes provide the incentive for reluctant imported tree frogs to start feeding.

Mice

Baby (pink) mice and preweaned mice can be fed sparingly to larger tree frogs. It is now the general consensus that a high mouse diet may not be good for the long-term health of tree frogs. Large frogs often become grotesquely obese on a mouse diet. This condition may be appealing to some frog keepers but, as with humans, fat and rich diets are not healthy for tree frogs in the long run and can lead to a number of diseases. A mouse once or twice a month, combined with a lower fat and lower protein diet including insects that have been fed vegetable matter, is probably a good basis for a healthy diet. It is very likely that in the wild, large frogs do occasionally ingest other verte-brates, probably smaller frogs.

Frogs

Some tree frogs will feed on other frogs. Indeed, for some species, such as members of the genus *Hemiphractus*, other frogs may constitute a significant component of the diet. But unless you work with frog-eating species, it is best to feed your tree frogs a nonfrog diet. When feeding tree frogs wild-collected frogs, you run the risk of exposing your animals to parasites and diseases.

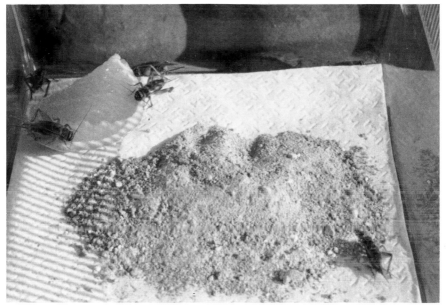

Everytime a frog eats, it swallows the gut contents of the insects it consumes. Feeding crickets on a high quality diet such as ground rodent chow with a wedge of orange as a water source is recommended prior to feeding insect eating frogs.

Feeding Commercially-raised Insects

It is now the general opinion, partially supported by research on lizards, that feeding food insects a high-quality diet is important and should be a key focus in the maintenance of frogs. Because of their opportunistic feeding habits, gray crickets are a good choice for gut-loading with a variety of high quality foods. Gut-loading is a process where food insects are fed a high quality diet with select vitamins and minerals. The insects with the desired food in their gut are then offered to the animals.

To do this, place crickets in a plastic terrarium 24 hours prior to feeding and offer them calcium-rich greens such as kale, collards, or mustard greens and finely chopped vegetables such as grated squashes, carrots, mixed vegetables, and occasional fruit. Sprinkle a small amount of powdered calcium carbonate on the food if you like, prior to offering it to the insects. Every third feeding, give crickets either a commercial cricket diet, powdered ground rodent chow, or food-processed grains such as oatmeal, barley, or sesame seed (in small amounts) mixed with calcium carbonate. A diet that is too rich or fatty will probably have a negative effect on amphibians and reptiles in the long run, so feeding crickets an exclusively commercial cricket diet is not necessarily the best idea, even though it is convenient.

Vitamin and mineral supplementation

You may wish to give vitamin and mineral supplementation to your tree frogs. For adult frogs the author supplements food insects once a week with a mix consisting of 50 percent calcium carbonate or calcium gluconate and 50 percent powdered multivitamin/mineral supplement such as Reptivite® or Herptivite® In addition, for approximately every cupful of mix, we recommend adding two human vitamin B-complex tablets, finely pulverized with a mortar and pestle. Additional B vitamins may be beneficial in helping frogs fight certain pathogens. Place a small amount of the mix in a jar and stir gently to coat the insects lightly prior to feeding. The key word here is *lightly*. You do not want so much mix that the crickets are white or beige with supplementation. They should appear lightly dusted. Because of their rapid growth, supplement the diets of juveniles and immature animals twice a week.

Metabolic bone disease and vitamin D3

We know that, like lizards, tree frogs that are fed a calcium and vitamin deficient diet will develop metabolic bone disease. In frogs the first symptom you notice is usually the inability to feed. By that time, the jaw bones have become soft and flexible. Other symptoms may include backbone deformities, sprawled hindlegs (the result of soft hip bones) and, in time, soft limbs. Another symptom is a drooping lower jaw or a lower jaw that grows beyond the end of the upper jaw. Hand feeding liquid calcium and vitamins with a syringe will generally reverse this disease if it has not progressed too far. A tree frog can also be assist-fed by placing prekilled crickets in its mouth, or force-fed with a syringe using Emeraid 2® (Lafeber's) or Exact® bird hand-feeding formula (Kaytee). The formula must be administered directly into the stomach and not in the mouth because frogs are built to swallow whole prey. You can do this with a large animal by gently inserting a tuberculin syringe containing feeding formula past its throat and into its stomach. In smaller species, you can gain access to the stomach by connecting fine tubing (such as model airplane fuel line tubing) to the end of a syringe filled with a liquified diet. This procedure requires experience, however, and is probably best left to the more specialized keeper.

One of the mysteries of tree frogs is their D3 requirements and whether D3 is significant in their ability to absorb calcium. The authors are currently carrying out research on this subject. There is little doubt that at least some tree frogs bask some of the time, usually toward dusk. For those species, exposure to UV rays may play a role in their synthesis of D3. On the other hand, there are many species that seldom or never expose themselves to sunlight; this fact eliminates the significance of UV rays for D3 synthesis in these frogs. In such cases, if D3 is significant in calcium absorption then it must have a dietary source.

Currently, the standard procedure is to supplement lightly the diet of tree frogs by feeding them crickets coated with a powdered commercial reptile vitamin/mineral supplement. Many herpetoculturists also provide full-spectrum lighting for their tree frogs. Larger tree frogs also can be offered occasional whole prey as a source of D3, such as baby mice or fuzzy mice, but mice should make up only a small portion of a treefrog's diet.

Hypervitaminosis

Hypervitaminosis in captive frogs has seldom been reported, partially because herpetoculturists usually do not associate a frog's symptoms with hypervitaminosis. If tree frogs are fed high levels of D3 and calcium, they may suffer kidney damage, which results in external signs such as water edema of the limbs and body. The authors suspect that other symptoms—such as calcium deposits in the internal organs, signs of metabolic bone disease, and other symptoms similar to those found in reptiles—may also occur in oversupplemented frogs. To avoid hypervitaminosis, feed your insects a high-quality diet that includes natural foods such as greens, vegetables, fruit, and a small percentage of grains and processed foods. In addition, remember to supplement your food insects LIGHTLY.

DO NOT OVER SUPPLEMENT TREE FROGS! Once a week light coating of insects with a powdered mix of two parts calcium to one part reptile vitamin/mineral supplement will be enough. High D3 and calcium supplements if fed too frequently can cause irreversible and fatal kidney disease. Visible symptoms can include water edema of the limbs and body, and lethargy.

Water

TREE FROGS SHOULD have clean water available at all times. You can offer it either in a shallow water container, such as a plastic storage box or a pet bowl, or through a water section designed in the vivarium. Change the water at least twice each week and whenever it is fouled with fecal matter. Wash the container once every week or two with an antibacterial dish detergent, and thoroughly rinse it before refilling it with water. The water should be high-quality water such as bottled drinking water or carbon-filtered water. It should be chlorine free; simply let water sit for 24 hours, and most of the chlorine will dissipate.

With frogs, bottled water or carbon-filtered water should be used unless tap water is of the highest quality. Tap water should be allowed to sit in containers to allow gases and chlorine to dissipate. If the water is treated with chloramine it should be treated accordingly.

Breeding Tree Frogs

F EW OF THE more common inexpensive tree frogs are currently worth breeding. It would be a better course to collect tadpoles on a regular basis and raise them indoors until they metamorphose into froglets. Greenhouse or screenhouse herpetoculture of common species is an excellent approach to captive propagation that can be accomplished where these frogs naturally occur. Management of wild treefrog populations may in many cases be a more viable option financially than indoor captive-breeding.

The opposite is the case with rarer tree frogs. Any serious frog herpetoculturist knows that rare or unusual frogs are available only sporadically and that every effort should be made to establish them in herpetoculture, in case they should not become available again. Some of the highly desirable species that come to mind are all of the Phyllomedusine tree frogs, any of the colorful tropical hylids such as *Hyla leucophyllata*, the gliding tree frogs of the genus *Rhacophorus*, and the crowned tree frog *Anotheca spinosa*.

The following are conditions for the successful breeding of tree frogs.
1. You must have one, and preferably several, healthy adult pairs.
2. They must have good weight but not be obese. Good muscle tone, such as is found in tree frogs raised in large enclosures that allows them to be active, is also desirable.

Rain Chambers

Rain chambers are extremely effective in encouraging various frog species to breed in captivity. They are particularly effective after a species has been given a winter rest—under cooler conditions for temperate species or a period of lower relative humidity and drier conditions for tropical species. Members of the genus *Litoria*, for example, breed readily after proper conditioning (cooler and drier)

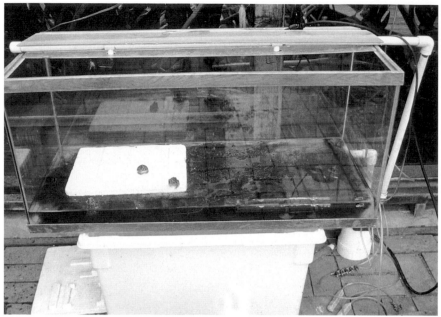

A simple rain chamber using an aquarium with glass cover, a submersible water pump, a PVC pipe adaptor, PVC pipe and irrigation system sprinkler heads (available in stores such as Home Depot). A simpler and effective alternative to sprinkler heads is to drill small holes along the length of the horizontal PVC sprinkler bar.

followed by exposure to rain chambers. Rain chambers can also be effective with tree frogs that have just been imported into this country, because they presumably have been collected at the onset of their breeding season. If they are healthy and appear to be in breeding condition (signified by nuptial pads in males and bulging abdomens in females), then introducing newly imported animals may pay off.

The following are two methods for building a rain chamber.
1. The rain chambers we have had the most success with are built using a 40- or 55-gallon aquarium with a screen top. Place a water pump on the bottom and link it to PVC pipe running up one side of the aquarium and along the length of the top or back side. Implant sprinkler heads in the PVC pipe about every 6 to 8 inches or drill multiple holes in the pipe. Add water to a depth of 3 to 6 inches, depending on the species. Place floating sections of Styrofoam® on top to cover about 25 percent of the surface, as well as some plants such

A Cuban tree frog (Osteopilus septentrionalis). This is the largest tree frog now found in the United States. Photo by Paul Freed.

A golden foam nest frog (Polypedates leucomystax). This tree frog is long-lived, and easy-to-breed. Photo by David Northcott, Nature's Lens.

25

A normal phase of the green tree frog (Hyla cinerea). Photo by D.B. Travis.

Rare "blue" axanthic green tree frog (Hyla cinerea). Photo by D.B. Travis.

Two color variations of the barking tree frog (Hyla gratiosa). Photo by Paul Freed.

A barking tree frog (Hyla gratiosa). Photo by David Northcott, Nature's Lens.

A gray tree frog (Hyla versicolor). These frogs have bright orange and black flash colors on their thighs. Photo by D.B. Travis.

A gliding tree frog (Rhacophorus nigropalmatus). Photo by David Northcott, Nature's Lens.

A pair of Australian red-eyed tree frogs (Litoria chloris) in amplexus. Photo by D.B. Travis.

Red-eyed tree frog (Agalychnis callidryas). Photo by Dennis Sheridan.

An egg mass of red-eyed tree frogs showing developing embryos. Photo by Michael Ready.

Tadpoles of red-eyed tree frogs (Agalychnis callidryas). Photo by Michael Ready.

A greenhouse raised White's tree frog. When raised indoors without exposure to natural light, these frogs often become bluish or brownish blue. Photo by D.B. Travis.

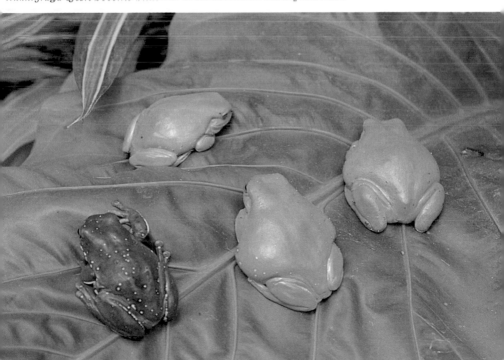

Color variation in White's tree frogs. Photo by D.B. Travis.

Albino Pacific tree frog (Hyla regilla). This morph will soon be available commercially.
Photo by D.B. Travis.

Australian white-lipped tree frog (Litoria infrafrenata). Photo by D.B. Travis.

as water hyacinth or hydroponically grown arrowhead plants. If you use enough plants, then Styrofoam® sections are not necessary.

2.   Another method for creating a rain chamber is to run a small water pump so that water flows above an aquarium with a screen top into a container resting on the top, such as a plastic storage container, with a finely perforated bottom. You can easily do this by using a drill with a small drill bit. You must give care to assure that the rate of outflow is equal to the rate of inflow, or the storage container may overfill and cause flooding.

Standard timers or timers that allow for multiple settings work well with rain chambers.

Misting

With several species of tropical tree frogs, extensive misting several times an evening can induce breeding. Misting can be done manually or with an automatic system.

Many of the tropical frogs species that lay eggs in foam nests or egg masses on plants above a water area (like many of the Phyllomedusine tree frogs) will breed after a prebreeding conditioning period of 3 to 8 weeks in which they are kept drier with no misting and water provided only in a dish of standing water. After this prebreeding conditioning they should be returned to a standard maintenance schedule that includes daily misting for 20 to 30 minutes three times a day, or exposure to a rain chamber for 2 to 4 hours daily. Phyllomedusine frogs, including the popular red-eye treefrog (*Agalychnis callidryas*) breed readily under this system, as do many other tropical forest frogs such as foam nest-building rhacophorids and various small tropical hylids such as the hourglass frog (*Hyla ebraccata*).

Loop Tapes as Additional Breeding Stimuli

Many frog species are sexually stimulated by the croaking (and other sounds) of male frogs of their own species. Anyone who has come upon breeding groups of frogs has experienced frog choruses by dozens, or even hundreds, of male frogs. Unfortunately, herpetoculturists usually can obtain only a few specimens of a particular species. Using a loop tape to record the sound of a male or males croaking allows you to play the tape while the frogs are in the breeding chamber and thereby provide additional stimulation for breeding.

Egg mass of red-eyed tree frogs on the side of a vivarium.

Breeding

None of the tree frogs mentioned in this book are particularly difficult to breed. The following are factors that will lead to successful breeding.

1. Breeding probability is increased when you keep several pairs of frogs together, at least during the breeding season.

2. Frogs that are conditioned for breeding should be healthy and have good weight but should not be grossly obese.

3. Winter cooling of 4 to 10 weeks, while keeping the frogs at a lower relative humidity, is recommended as conditioning prior to breeding.

4. Time cooling so that the frogs are exposed to real or simulated rain during barometric low-pressure conditions, such as when a storm is coming. This increases the probability of breeding.

5. Provide large enclosures with large water areas. Frog spawns tend to be large, and if the frogs breed in a small water area the risk is high that eggs or tadpoles will die because of reduced oxygen in the water. Adding water later can be risky unless you have allowed water to sit and age for several days.

*A shallow water container is placed under the egg mass to c[...]
frog tadpoles as they drop.*

A Standard Procedure for Breeding Tree Frogs

If you are considering breeding tree frogs, you should fir[...]
on their life histories and the climatic patterns of their ar[...]
As rough guidelines for breeding you will find the followin[...]

1. **Temperate tree frogs:** They should be kept cooler and[...]
misting) for one to two months during the winter. How cool y[...]
their vivarium should be determined by the climatic toleranc[...]
species you are keeping. Usually cooling into the 60s F(daytin[...]
50s F(nighttime) should be adequate for most temperate speci[...]
photoperiod during the cooling period should be only 10 hours[...]
per 24 hours.

After the cooling period, feed the frogs well for two to three we[...]
then place pairs in a rain chamber, setting the timer for the water[...]
pump to run from 6 p.m. to 10 p.m. Do this for several days and[...]
breeding will usually occur within a week if your frogs are ready to[...]
breed. Remember that many species may breed a second and even[...]
third time if they have been fed well for three weeks or more before[...]
rain-chamber exposure.

2. Tropical tree frogs: As a general rule, many tropical species of tree frogs will breed if kept at a lower relative humidity (no misting) and slightly cooler (5 to 8 degrees F), then fed well for a couple of weeks and exposed to daily misting or a rain chamber for several hours. Expose frogs to misting or a rain-chamber in the early evening for up to five days with species from dry areas and up to three weeks with tropical rainforest species; however, you should remove them from the chamber as soon as breeding has occurred. Breeding typically occurs in the evening during or after the period of "rain." Be careful not to overdo the use of rain-chambers, because the frogs may become stressed after excessive exposure and succumb to disease. Carefully monitor frogs, their color, and the condition of their skin when they are in rain-chambers. If your frogs look off color or in any way ill, return them to normal conditions immediately, particularly if they show no signs of breeding behavior.

Rearing Tadpoles

Tadpoles are very sensitive to water conditions and changes in water conditions. During the first days following hatching, it is best to raise them in the rain-chamber tank. Later you can transfer them to rearing tanks. Always use dechlorinated or dechloraminated water when rearing tadpoles. You also should allow the water to age for at least 24 hours before use, so that dissolved gases may escape. Introducing warm water from the tap into a tank of tadpoles can, with some species, result in gas-bubble disease. (Dissolved gases at higher temperature and higher concentration than that of the tadpole's body can penetrate its skin and accumulate, forming a subcutaneous gas bubble that will usually prove fatal.) Tadpoles that float or cannot swim toward the bottom of their enclosures are usually the victims of gas-bubble disease.

Having large tanks with aged high-quality water is a requirement for successfully rearing tree frog tadpoles. The pH of the water should be slightly alkaline, with most species 7.2 to 7.4. Acid water can be tolerated by only a few species. If you have greenhouse facilities, you can employ children's wading pools, readily available during the summer months in department stores, or plastic watering troughs such as those produced by Rubbermaid® for tadpole rearing or conditioning water. The authors add carbon-filtered water and water hyacinth and water lettuce to these troughs, which are kept in greenhouses. These

Large aquaria are required if large numbers of tadpoles are to be raised indoors.

plants will maintain high water quality while the tadpoles are raised. Later they will provide climbing areas for the emerging froglets.

Whenever you change tadpole water, attempt to match the temperature of the tadpole water and to maintain similar purity and pH as the original setup water. Spreading out tadpoles in several tanks and keeping them at moderate densities (5 per gallon) will increase your chances of success.

Indoors, the best filtering systems are air pump driven biological foam filters. They will allow easy cleaning of the filters while preventing the risk of tadpoles being sucked into a motor-driven filter. Box filters can be used safely if packed with enough floss that tadpoles cannot become trapped in the box. Undergravel filters also work well, but they present the risks of overloading the filter with biological waste. Aquatic plants if provided with enough light are also beneficial. We use water hyacinth in sunlit greenhouses but other species can be employed. Leafy species may also be eaten by the tadpoles. You can heat the tadpole rearing tanks with submersible heaters, and if you keep them indoors you should light them with overhead fluorescent full-spectrum lighting for 12 to 14 hours per day.

Feeding tadpoles

Most tree frog tadpoles will feed on commercial fish diets. As a rule, a basic fish flake such as Tetramin® and spirulina containing flakes such as Tetra Spirulina Flakes® are good food sources for tree frog tadpoles. Sera Micron,® a powdered algae-containing diet, is a worthwhile dietary supplement, particularly for small tadpoles. Use a varied diet such as spirulina flakes and standard flake food when possible. Do not feed excessively or you risk fouling the water and threatening the lives of your tadpoles. Usually a light feeding two or three times daily will result in rapid growth. Monitor water conditions and change water as needed.

Water tests

A common complaint of aspiring frog breeders is "I don't know what happened; the tadpoles were doing fine, and then all of a sudden they started dying in mass." The usual reason for this phenomenon is that as tadpoles grow larger, you give them more food, and although everything seems like it's the same, in fact more food is eaten and therefore more wastes are produced. Sudden large scale tadpole deaths are usually the result of changes in water quality, often a build up of nitrates and ammonia. Besides regular 10 percent partial water changes (once or twice a week in most cases), the water should be tested on a regular basis for ammonia and pH. If you are using a method of pool rearing by which all you do is add water when needed, you also should test the water for hardness.

Metamorphosing Froglets

As tadpoles grow they initially get larger; then their hindlimbs emerge, followed by the forelimbs as the head and mouth change into a froglet mouth. The tail during this process is reabsorbed. Once it becomes a froglet, a tree frog will exhaust itself and drown if it does not have access to climbing areas. It is critical at the time of metamorphosis to provide climbing areas that offer easy access from the water to surface plants. Plants that grow well in water, such as arrowhead plants, pothos, and chinese evergreen will work in indoor setups, as will partially submerged rocks, freshwater driftwood, or acrylic or glass ramps attached with silicone to the bottom of the enclosure. The message here is: provide a climbing area that allows froglets to leave the water.

Handling

Tree frogs are primarily animals to be observed and not handled. No frogs like to be petted by dry, rough human hands. If you feel a compulsion to pet frogs, wash your hands with clean water and wet your hand first, but this is generally not recommended. You can allow some of the calmer tree frogs to climb and rest on a hand, but most species will not remain in place for any length of time and will eventually jump off. The one exception is White's tree frogs, particularly adults. They tend to be placid and will remain on a hand for long periods prior to any intentions of jumping. For this reason, along with the hardiness characteristic of this species we rank White's tree frog as the best and most recommended tree frog pet. We recommend that no children be allowed to handle frogs without parental supervision. Tree frogs can hop out of young hands and escape. There are also problems of hygiene with frog handling. Children should be told not to put fingers in their mouths or to rub their eyes during or after handling a frog. They should be told to wash their hands immediately after handling any frog, preferably with a bactericidal soap.

NOTES ON POPULAR SPECIES

Cuban Tree Frog *(Osteopilus septentrionalis)*

The Cuban tree frog an introduced species, is now well established in South Florida. It is the largest tree frog now existing in the United States.

Size: Males are 1 1/2 to 3 1/2 inches. Females grow up to 5 inches, very rarely larger.

Distribution: South Florida, Cuba and the Isle of Pines, the Bahamas and Cayman Islands; introduced on Puerto Rico and St. Croix

Sexing: Male's are smaller, with a darker throat and nuptial pads in breeding

Care and maintenance: As long as it is kept warm enough (at temperatures in the upper 70s to low 80s in the day, lows in the 70s at night), this is a relatively easy species to keep. It can be maintained like White's tree frogs and will also consume larger prey such as baby mice when mature.

Breeding: Cuban tree frogs breed easily after a slight winter cooling and are very prolific. Their egg masses consist of up to 2,000 eggs. The tadpoles hatch in 24 to 48 hours and can be fed on tropical fish flakes such as Tetramin® staple diet. They will metamorphose in 6 to 8 weeks. Sexual maturity is reached by one year. There is currently no need to captive breed this common and inexpensive frog.

Note: Do not keep this frog with smaller animals. It will make a meal of them. Its skin secretions are quite noxious, so care should be given not to rub eyes during or after handling them.

Green Tree Frog *(Hyla cinerea)*

The green tree frog is a delightful United States species that is attractive, readily available, and easy to keep.

Size: 1 1/4 to 2 1/4 inches

Distribution: Wide ranging. Delaware south along the coastal plain into Florida and west to Texas, north through central Arkansas and western Tennessee to Illinois.

Sexing: Mature males have a darker, dirty-yellow throat.

Variation: Some individuals have a fair amount of golden yellow spotting. Others have wide silvery-white side stripes that are also very appealing. Both of the above variations may be more widespread among certain populations. Selective breeding for yellow spotting and wide stripes could result in some spectacular animals in the future. Recently an axanthic specimen was collected that is an intense light blue. It was purchased (courtesy of Glades Herp) by Robert Mailloux and has been successfully bred to normal animals. An F2 generation is in the works and, depending on the genetics of this trait, sky-blue colored green tree frogs may one day be available in herpetoculture.

Care and maintenance: Similar to that of White's tree frog, but a naturalistic vivarium is recommended. Established specimens lie on plants and make nice vivarium displays. Males tend to call whenever a low-pressure system moves in and can be noisy.

Breeding: This is not a difficult species to breed if it is cooled down during the winter. At least two males and an equal number of females can be kept together. Raised temperatures, drops in barometric pressure, and rain chambers will condition these frogs for breeding. About 700 eggs are laid in a clutch, and more than one clutch can be laid per season. The tadpole stage lasts around 35 days. Tadpoles can be raised easily on a standard fish flake diet. The tiny froglets will feed on week-old crickets. Under optimal conditions, sexual maturity is reached in less than a year.

Note: In the wild, there are areas in which this species hybridizes with the barking tree frog.

Barking Tree Frog *(Hyla gratiosa)*

The barking tree frog is one of the prettiest of the United States species. Its large, squat body and attractive colors and patterns make this one of the most desirable of the U.S. tree frogs.

Size: 2 to 2 3/4 inches

Distribution: North Carolina to south Florida and eastern Louisiana. There are also colonies in Delaware, Maryland, Kentucky, Tennessee, and Virginia.

Longevity: 7 years or more

Sexing: Males have a loose greenish-yellow throat. The majority of animals sold in pet stores are collected during breeding and are males.

Care and Maintenance: The same general care as for *Hyla cinerea*. Under optimal conditions of moderate warmth and moderate relative humidity, this species will rest on leaves, sides of the enclosures, and other surfaces. Under less than optimal conditions (too dry, too cool, too warm), this species will burrow under landscape structures or just beneath the surface of the substrate. In spite of what several other authors have written, the barking tree frog is not always an easy species to keep on a long-term basis. One reason is that collected animals stored in crowded conditions prior to distribution may become infested by parasites. Matching natural climatic cycles and environmental conditions may be necessary for long-term survival in captivity.

Breeding: This species should be bred commercially. It certainly ranks among the best tree frogs, and it has many of the physical characteristics that make frogs appealing: dumpy appearance, attractive coloration, and good display potential (when they don't hide). Unfortunately, we have not attempted to breed this species and could not find a captive breeding record for it. But following a period of cooling, the barking tree frog should breed if it is exposed to rain and decreased barometric pressure.

Gray tree frogs *(Hyla chrysoscelis* and *Hyla versicolor)*

Gray tree frogs are commonly available in the spring, when they are collected during breeding aggregations. These two species, which are similar in appearance but can be distinguished by their calls (*chrysoscelis* fast trill, *versicolor* slow trill), have an appealing cryptic beauty: they are marbled in gray or with shades of green or a pale, almost white coloration. Their color will change, depending on a number of factors, including temperature and exposure to light. In addition these frogs have bright orange and black flash colors on their thighs. Genetically, *chrysoscelis* is diploid, whereas *versicolor* is tetraploid (twice the number of chromosome pairs). All and all, gray tree frogs are very pretty animals that display well in a planted vivarium. They can be kept like green tree frogs but fare best over the long term if they are exposed to cooler winter temperatures (50s and 60s), at least at night, for one to two months.

Size: 1 1/4 to 2 3/8 inches

Sexing: Males have a darker yellowish throat.

Longevity: 7 years or more

Care and Maintenance: Similar to that of the green tree frog but requires cool winter temperatures in the 50s (will tolerate 40s) for one to two months for breeeding and greater longevity.

Breeding: If they were to become less common, the gray tree frogs would be a species worth breeding. Greenhouse environments with pools set up within their range of distribution would be the recommended procedure for large scale breeding. *Hyla versicolor* has been bred indoors. Gray tree froglets display digital fluttering of the hind middle digits when feeding.

Golden foam nest frogs *(Polypedates leucomystax)*

Golden foam nest frogs used to be imported regularly from Southeast Asia. If they are healthy when first obtained, they are a hardy, long-lived, and easy-to-breed frog. Large females can have an even golden color that is very attractive.

Size: Males 2 3/4 inches; large females up to four inches

Longevity: 6 years or more

Distribution: Southeast Asia and introduced in several areas

Care: Similar to that of White's tree frog, but these frogs are not tolerant of low temperatures or low relative humidity. They are best kept in naturalistic tropical-forest vivaria with daytime temperatures in the upper 70s to low 80s. Minimum temperatures should be in the low 70s. Once established, these frogs make good display animals.

Breeding: Under the dry/ wet-cycle method, this species breeds readily in captivity. The female creates foam nests and lays about 175 eggs, which hatch in three to four days. Several clutches can be laid per year. This is a prolific tree frog. The tadpoles should be able to fall into an underlying container of water. They can be raised on tropical fish flake food and will metamorphose at between one and three

A male green tree frog calling. Photo by Bill Love.

months. The froglets are easily raised with standard tadpole-rearing methods.

Gliding tree frogs *(Rhacophorus nigropalmatus* and *R. rheinwardtii)*

These large Asian tree frogs rank among the more beautiful tree frogs because of their brightly colored webbing and sides. Unfortunately, imported specimens are typically thin, weak, highly parasitized, and with varying numbers of dorsal sores. Every effort should be made to establish these beautiful tree frogs in captivity.

Size: Up to 3½ inches (8.9 cm)

Care and Maintenance: These high-mortality tree frogs can be established by using the procedures set forth in this book. Treatment with Flagyl® and Baytril® combined with handfeeding can work miracles. Once established, these species can be kept like red-eyed tree frogs.

Larger plants such as Chinese evergreens are recommended as perching and possible breeding areas.

Breeding: Not bred in captivity to our knowledge but can probably be bred like red-eyed tree frogs or foam-nest frogs, using a similar method.

Australian red-eyed tree frog *(Litoria chloris)*

No one can quite remember when these tree frogs first became available. Froglets captive-bred in Europe were offered by some of the large dealers about ten years ago, but there are reports of animals being offered in the early 1980s. Since then, this species has been intermittently available as captive-bred froglets. The authors have bred this species on a number of occasions, and they are becoming more regularly available. (At least 1,000 froglets now are offered through the pet trade every year.) Although not as attractive as Central American red-eyed tree frogs, these frogs have bright yellow-orange hands and feet, and their eyes are probably best described as having orange or red-edged irises. It is probable that some Australian populations have more extensive red irises than others.

These tree frogs can be maintained and bred under conditions similar to those of White's tree frogs, but they are generally less tolerant of low relative humidity and temperature extremes than White's tree frogs.

Size: Up to 2$\frac{1}{2}$ inches

Males: Slightly smaller than females with yellowish throat.

Distribution: Australia

Growth: Under optimal rearing conditions, this species becomes sexually mature by 9 months.

Breeding: If kept slightly cooler and drier for 8 weeks, then introduced into a rain chamber, this species will breed readily. The authors have obtained as many as 5 clutches in an extended breeding season by placing pairs in a rain chamber every 4 weeks. Australian red-eyed tree frogs are prolific and lay around 500 eggs per clutch. They should be well fed and kept relatively dry between clutches. The tadpoles hatch in 2 days and are easily raised on Tetramin® Staple tropical fish flakes. The froglets emerge after 4 weeks.

Diseases and Disorders

HEALTHY FROGS CAN fight off a wide range of potential pathogens, and the first consideration of the herpetoculturist should be to provide optimal conditions for minimizing stress and allowing a frog's immune system to function properly. To do so, you must keep your frogs at the relative humidity and temperature range required by their particular species. You should also design their vivarium to provide the right kind of landscaping in the form of proper substrates, shelters, and plants. Equally important is to select frogs that initially appear to be potentially healthy. Despite optimal conditions, tree frogs may exhibit symptoms of disease. The following are common diseases that can be readily treated by herpetoculturists or veterinarians.

Obesity

Captive tree frogs that are overfed and inactive can become grossly obese. This is particularly true of White's tree frogs fed large amounts of pink mice or allowed to stuff themselves daily. As with humans, obese tree frogs typically have shortened lifespans. In White's tree frogs, the fatty deposits around the head can become so great that they will cover the eyes and essentially blind the animal. Gradually cutting back on the amount of food offered and providing large vivaria that allow frogs to be active will help reverse obesity. Plumpness may look cute but it is not necessarily healthy.

Internal Parasites

Nematodes

Frogs can harbor nematode worms, and any weight loss while the feces appear more or less formed should direct the herpetoculturist to the possibility of nematodes. Ideally a fecal exam should be performed, but success also has been had by simply treating frogs orally with Panacur® (fenbendazole) orally at 50 to 75 mg/kg. Repeat in 7 days.

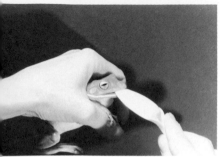
The use of an inverted plastic spoon can be used to open the mouth of larger tree frogs.

The use of a plastic wedge cut from a deli cup can be used to open the mouth of smaller frogs.

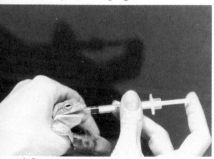
Administering liquid metronidazole orally with a syringe to a white-lipped treefrog.

Injecting a White's tree frog subcutaneously with Baytril® (enrofloxacin).

Flagellate protozoans

Runny and or bloody feces can be caused by flagellate protozoans. A fecal exam should be performed by a veterinarian if possible (see *Understanding Reptile Parasites* by Roger Klingenberg). Flagellate protozoans can be treated with Flagyl® (metronidazole) administered orally, directly in the stomach at a dosage of 50 mg/kg.

Sores and Injuries

It is not uncommon for imported tree frogs to have rubbed snouts, skin sores, and physical injuries. The authors have had good success in treating these problems by injecting Baytril® (enrofloxacin) in the ventral area at a dosage of 10 mg/kg, repeated every 48 hours for up to as many as 14 days. With imported frogs, the authors also administer Flagyl® which is antibiotic to anaerobic bacteria.

Clouded eyes

In most cases, clouded eyes occur in imported frogs. This disease is often caused by trauma to the eyes or an immune-system failure or absorption of toxins. You can usually treat this by keeping the frogs in simple vivaria with paper towel as a substrate, and administering Baytril® (enrofloxacin), injecting it ventrally (see previous section).

A poor diet is another cause of clouded eyes. As a rule, a lean insect diet is preferable to fatty diets such as pink mice. Dirty water or water that has a high ammonia and urate content can also cause clouding of the eyes.

Female Indonesian White's tree frog with extremely developed supratympanic ridges. The eyes are nearly covered over. This animal eventually died.

Bacterial infections

Stressed frogs may become victims of bacterial infections, such as *Pseudomonas* infections, that result in sores and other symptoms. Smears from sores can be cultured and tested for antibiotic sensitivity. Most frogs can absorb water-soluble antibiotics through their skin, so one efficient method of treating large numbers of frogs is spraying them with an appropriately diluted antibiotic solution once or twice daily, as needed. Care must be given by those in charge of administering antibiotics to avoid inhaling antibiotic spray or aerosol. Injectable antibiotics also work well and are recommended in serious cases.

See Wright, K.M. 1996, "Amphibian Husbandry and Medicine" in *Reptile Medicine and Surgery*, edited by D. Mader, W.B. Saunders Company.

Red leg

Red leg is a general term for a disease caused by *Aeromonas*. Unsanitary conditions, prolonged exposure to cold conditions, overcrowding, and other factors that lead to stress contribute to red leg.

Symptoms include listlessness, bloating, lack of appetite, and the reddish appearance of the underside of the thighs and belly, which is caused by enlarged and broken capillaries resulting in subcutaneous bleeding. Treatment with tetracycline administered orally at 50 mg/kg twice a day should be initiated immediately. Additional injectable antibiotics are also recommended. See Wright 1996 for additional information.

Water edema of the limbs and body

If a tree frog looks like it is bloated with water, particularly in its limbs, then there is a good chance that your frog may suffer from kidney disease. This is not usually reversible and is best prevented through proper husbandry. It is important to keep your frog's water clean at all times so that it does not reabsorb wastes such as urine from its water container. Other factors that may contribute to kidney disease include other diseases, diets that are too rich (such as an exclusive pink-mouse diet), and excessive calcium and D3 supplementation.

Toxing out

Frogs can absorb water substances from their environment and from water particularly through the ventral (belly skin). Ammonia, urates, toxins (including frog toxins) can be absorbed by frogs causing convulsions, hind leg extensions, bloating, and eye clouding. Keeping frog environments clean is essential for long term survival. Frogs with "toxing out" symptoms can sometimes be treated by soaking them in low levels of clean water for several hours.

Drying out

Escaped tree frogs are often found on the verge of death. To rehydrate, first gently remove with a moist Q-tip® any dust or hair that might be covering the skin. Then place the frog in a pan of shallow water, no more than half the height of the frog when at rest inside a secure enclosure. Dehydrated frogs are often too weak to climb out of deep water and will drown.

See page 20 for Metabolic Bone Disease and Vitamin D3

Part II
The Red-eyed Tree Frog
(Agalychnis callidryas)

By
Drew W. Ready

Introduction

THE RAIN FORESTS of Central America are home to some of the most interesting and beautiful plants and animals on this earth. Among the orchids, bromediads, broad-leafed plants, and tangles of tropical vines there lives a tree frog whose splendor and magnificence are unsurpassed. It is *Agalychnis callidryas*, the red-eyed tree frog.

This tree frog was originally described by Cope in 1862, and he gave the species a name that would forever identify it for its extraordinary resplendence. The specific name, *callidryas,* is a derivative of the Greek words *kallos,* meaning "beautiful," and *dryas,* meaning "tree nymph"; hence it is a perfect name for this frog: the beautiful tree nymph.

Few red-eyed tree frogs were imported prior to the mid to late 1980s, when United States importers began receiving regular shipments of reptiles and amphibians from the Central American country, Honduras. The shipments of frogs and other "herps" came in by the hundreds. Along with red-eyed tree frogs, forest chameleons *(Corytophanes cristatus),* conchead lizards *(Laemanctus longipes),* emerald swifts *(Sceloporus malachiticus),* masked tree frogs *(Smilisca baudini),* turnip tail geckos *(Thecadactylus rapicaudus),* palm salamanders *(Bolitoglossa sp.)*, and an assortment of other species became available to the general public through the pet trade.

It was rumored for some time that Honduras would be closing its doors to all exportation, and finally in the late 1980s all Honduran herp shipments ceased. Within two years, very few red-eyed tree frogs remained in captivity. I found that there were two primary reasons for this: the first was a lack of detailed, quality husbandry information available on this species, and the second was simple neglect. By 1990, of the thousands of red-eyed tree frogs imported from Honduras I found that less than a hundred remained in U.S. collections.

Fortunately for us frog enthusiasts, there have been recent shipments of red-eyed tree frogs entering the United States from Guatemala and Nicaragua, and it seems that they are again being collected and imported in large numbers.

General Information

Taxonomy

The red-eyed tree frog is a member of the family *Hylidae* of the order *Anura* and within the class *Amphibia*. The family *Hylidae* comprises all true tree frogs and is made up of many subfamilies. Red-eyed tree frogs exist within the subfamily *Phyllomedusinae*, in which there are six genera and forty-two recognized species. The genus of the red-eyed tree frog, *Agalychnis*, is shared with seven other species.

The other species of the genus include: *Agalychnis annae, A. calcarifer, A. craspedopus, A. litodryas, A. moreletii, A. saltator,* and *A. spurrelli. Agalychnis callidryas* is distinguished from all other species of the genus by its light to dark blue or brown flanks (or sides) with vertical white to yellow bars. As of today, *A. callidryas* is the only species of this genus that is regularly imported for the pet trade in the United States.

Description

Males of this species reach a maximum snout-to-vent length of 2.2 inches (56 mm). Females, which are larger, can reach a snout-to-vent length of more than 2.5 inches (70mm). Color and size vary, depending on geographic location. Red-eyes from the northernmost part of their range (Southern Mexico and Guatemala) are the smallest and usually display light blue flanks; those from more southern parts (Nicaragua and Costa Rica) tend to be larger in size and display flanks colored dark blue. The red-eye tree frog's dorsum, or back, is green. Variations on the shade of green are also geographically determined. Some red-eyes have small white spots on their dorsal surface. Their venters, or bellies, are creamy white, and their feet are shades of yellow to orange.

The vertical pupil is uncommon in the eyes of hylids, but it is a characteristic that all members of the Phyllomedusine subfamily exhibit. The red eye is shared with other members of the genus and is an attribute of other species of hylids, such as the Australian tree frog, *Litoria chloris*. It is theorized that the brilliant coloration or flash markings of this species exist to startle and ward off predators.

Distribution

The red-eyed tree frog is found from southern Mexico south to eastern Panama. It is a species that dwells in tropical lowland rain forest, although it has also been located on the upward slopes of tropical mountain regions. Because of the mass destruction of Central American rain forest habitat and the recent decline of many amphibian populations, it is not known whether or not these frogs still exist in areas defined by previous type localities.

Behavioral Characteristics

RED-EYED TREE FROGS are primarily arboreal and nocturnal, sleeping in the forest canopy during the day. As day turns to night, the frogs awake, their colors in full display, to walk about and hunt for food. The red-eyed tree frog is considered to be exclusively insectivorous, taking advantage of the huge abundance of insects of the forest canopy. As the light of morning approaches, the frogs search out a resting spot—a palm frond, a *Philodendron* leaf, or a bromeliad—to call home for the day. Once they have found a suitable resting site, they bring in their arms and legs tight to their bodies, close their eyes, and virtually disappear against the foliage.

Breeding occurs at the onset of the rainy season. As depressions in the ground fill up with rain water and form small pools, the red-eyed tree frog descends from the canopy to find a mate. From branches and vines above these temporary ponds, males emit a series of calls in anticipation of attracting responsive females. Once a female approaches a male, or a male finds a female, he climbs on her back and proceeds to clasp her. If the female is receptive she then explores for a suitable site or sites in which to deposit her eggs. Usually a large leaf a few feet above the water will do, but clutches of eggs have also been found on vines, branches, and tree trunks above or near water.

The female releases the eggs in a gelatinous mass, and they are fertilized by the clinging male. Clutches contain on average about fifty eggs, although clutches of from fourteen to one-hundred and eight eggs have been noted. The developing tadpoles wriggle themselves about, rupture the enveloping membrane, and fall into the water within six to ten days. The tadpoles forage for food within the pool and complete metamorphosis in from forty to eighty days. The emerging froglets are usually brownish in color and lack the characteristic red pigment in their eyes. The striking colors are acquired as the tree frog develops.

Care in Captivity

Selecting Healthy Tree Frogs

When you first see a red-eyed tree frog, you may find it very difficult to resist the impulse to purchase the animal without taking the steps necessary to make sure that the frog is in good health and has not succumbed to the stresses of captivity. It is also important that you first acquire the appropriate equipment and know-how.

By the time most wild-caught amphibians reach a dealer, they have traveled through many hands and will have arrived malnourished and stressed. You should select animals with no visible discoloration. The tree frogs, if they have been kept and shipped properly, should have a healthy body weight; no bone outlines should be visible. During transport these frogs are shipped in small containers in which they easily damage their snouts. Avoid any frogs with discoloration or rawness of the snout (and possibly suggest that they be treated immediately by the dealer).

Examine the entire animal, looking for any signs of infection. Sick animals appear thin and are often awake during daylight hours.

It is best to purchase captive-bred amphibians whenever possible. They lack the parasites of wild-caught animals and there is no need to acclimate them to captivity. Captive-bred stock are at the present moment more prevalent in pet stores than they ever have been. I am hopeful that as the interest in keeping and breeding amphibians develops, we will see the number of captive-produced tree frogs in the market increase further, easing the pressure that collecting has put on wild populations.

Secondary Sex Characteristics

Sexing the red-eyed tree frog is easily accomplished when you are selecting from a large group. Males are much smaller than females,

A naturalistic vivarium suitable for keeping tree frogs.

attaining a maximum length of only 2.2 inches (56 mm). Adult females are larger, reaching lengths upwards of 2.5 inches (70 mm). With juveniles and froglets it seems to be the luck of the draw, although some females can be determined by their more truncate snouts.

Housing

A CCLIMATIZATION IS ONE of the most important factors in keeping frogs. Animals taken from the wild do not acclimate well to small enclosures. You can use a tall thirty-gallon terrarium to create a vivarium that provides a small group of red-eyes with the space they need. Custom-built vivaria for arboreal frogs are even better. Your vivarium should have a top that is half glass and half screen, to assure adequate ventilation and proper humidity. Red-eyes should be housed in nothing smaller than a tall twenty-gallon terrarium. Other authors have suggested smaller setups, but tree frogs need space, especially vertical space, and animals housed in smaller vivaria may eventually succumb to the stresses of confinement.

Temperature, Humidity, and Water Requirements

The optimum temperature for red-eyed tree frogs ranges between 60 and 85 degrees Fahrenheit (approximately 15 to 30 degrees Celsius). Constant exposure to the extremes of this range may cause health problems.

There are two common practices for keeping the enclosure within the required temperature range. The first is to keep the room in which the animals are housed within an ambient temperature range, thereby assuring that the vivarium remains at the desired temperatures. Because the temperature in some rooms fluctuates greatly or may become too cool or too hot, heating and cooling the setup directly is a better method.

Under-the-tank heat elements work very well. If this is not a convenient method for you, or if it does not supply enough heat, you can place low-wattage incandescent light bulbs outside the enclosure to increase the temperature. Low-wattage ceramic heat elements that can be screwed into normal incandescent fixtures also provide a good source of heat. But because vivaria can heat up fast, maintain several inches between the heat source and the top of the vivarium.

Keeping a room adequately cool in the summer months can also pose problems for tree frog enthusiasts. Vivaria should never get direct sunlight in the warmer months. Keeping the shades (or blinds, shutters, or draperies) closed and the windows open in a room will greatly reduce the ambient temperature. If vivarium temperatures rise above 90 degrees, turn off the lights, as even fluorescent lighting can warm the vivarium. You can turn the lights on again after the heat of the day has passed. You also can use small utility fans to circulate cooler air into the vivarium, and an occasional misting of the enclosure will reduce its temperature.

You should maintain the vivarium's humidity levels at between 30 and 50 percent during the dry cycle (when breeding is not being induced). Constant humidity levels higher than 80 percent can cause health problems in your frogs. When you have provided them with a proper water section and half-screen /half-glass top, all you need to do is give the vivarium a light misting a couple of times each week to maintain the proper humidity level.

Create a small water area by sectioning a corner of the vivarium with a small piece of glass attached with aquarium silicone; otherwise a water dish should be accessible at all times. It is essential to make clean water always available to this species. At night, red-eyes find their way to the water and sit with their posteriors submerged in order to achieve rehydration. Most tap water is potentially toxic to frogs; therefore, you must not use water from the tap unless it has been filtered extensively.

The water should also be dechlorinated and dechloramined, which you can do by using the commercial product Amquel® available in most aquarium stores. Bottled or filtered water (or a combination of the two) works best. You must change the water in red-eye vivaria frequently because the frogs naturally defecate and urinate in the water section. Filtration devices are not recommended, because they do not keep the water as clean as a regular water change. Bear in mind that a key to good vivarium design and function is keeping the setup simple and natural.

Plants for Vivarium Design

The best design strategy for the red-eyed tree frog, as with most captive amphibians, is to create a naturalistic vivarium. Simulation of the animals' natural habitat has long been known to ease the stress of captivity and to facilitate acclimation. I use a three- to five-inch substrate of orchid bark. The vivarium is best landscaped with broad-leafed plants of the aroid family, including *Philodendron*, *Anthurium*, and *Monstera* species. You can find these plants at most good nurseries, and you can obtain more exotic species through specialty greenhouses and mail-order nurseries that specialize in tropical plants.

Planted terrariums are also an option, but you must make good drainage available. Plants left in pots and sunken into a bark substrate allow for easy maintenance, and the vivarium will still very much resemble a little rain forest. You can mount slabs of cork bark on the side of the vivarium by attaching a piece of string to the back side of the cork as you would a framed picture. You can find suction cups with a small mounting bracket attached at most nurseries and hardware stores. Stick the suction cup against the glass and mount the cork bark. This design element is aesthetically pleasing and allows the vivarium to resemble a treelike dwelling. The more you understand about the habitat from which the red-eyed tree frog originates, the better you can meet its needs in captivity.

Lighting

It is still debated whether or not full-spectrum lighting is a necessity for these nocturnal tree frogs. It is known, however, that planted vivaria must have lighting that replicates natural sunlight. Full-spectrum fluorescent bulbs are readily available and provide plants with the needed spectrum of light. Because one bulb is seldom sufficient for many plants, two or more fluorescent bulbs are the optimum.

The red-eyed tree frog should be given a light cycle of twelve hours on and twelve hours off. You can accomplish this easily by using appliance timers, which are available at most hardware stores. This automation allows for a more exact light cycle and will save you the task of turning your lights off and on every day. You can employ a dark blue or red incandescent light bulb at night to observe these amazing creatures as they awake and move about the enclosure. In the cooler months, you can use low-wattage (around 25 watts) full-spectrum incandescent bulbs to add light and warmth, but you should always be careful to avoid harmful temperatures.

Feeding

CRICKETS, THE STAPLE diet for many captive reptiles and amphibians, work quite well for feeding red-eyed tree frogs. But you should remember that a varied diet is the best. For years, I have fed my frogs crickets and houseflies without problems, but you must follow a few steps to assure that your frogs receive proper nutrition. Rather than feeding them store-bought crickets directly, it is better first to feed the insects a high-nutrient load. You can store the insects in a ten-gallon aquarium or similar container. Egg crates and torn brown bags work well in the container for crickets to hide in and defecate on. You can feed the crickets a variety of foods, but carrots, kale, oranges, monkey chow or trout chow, chicken mash, and pulverized fish foods (small percent of total diet) seem to work best.

When offering your frogs the crickets, dust the insects once a week with high-quality vitamin and calcium supplements, which are available from most herp dealers. Rather than letting the crickets run free about the frog vivarium, place them in bowls or similar containers. This method tends to keep the supplements on the crickets longer, keeps them out of water, and ensures that your frogs do not consume bark, soil, or any other nonfood material. Most tree frogs have no problem eating from these bowls. It is best to feed them two to three times per week, supplying them with only enough food for a couple of days at each feeding.

A male adult red-eyed tree frog (Agalychnis callidryas).

Breeding in Captivity

IF YOU FOLLOW all of the previous husbandry procedures, it won't be long until you, as well as your frogs, will be interested in breeding. Most of the time it is best to keep the vivarium environment moderately dry. A light misting a couple of times each week is all that is necessary to assure the ideal humidity. With the ability to manipulate warm-and cool and wet-and-dry cycles within the vivarium, you can breed red-eyes at various times of the year; however, it is best to avoid any breeding or tadpole-rearing activity during the cold winter months.

The warming temperatures and frequent barometric instability of mid-to-late spring is an optimum time to breed this species. Red-eyes are a bit more listless and feed less during the cooler winter months. As winter turns to spring and the weather starts to warm up, the frogs become more active and the males may even start calling. Warm temperatures, spring rains, and the changes in barometric pressure induce breeding activity, but without simulated rain the frogs will not breed.

It is important to make preparations well in advance for all breeding and rearing necessities. Tall, medium-to large sizes of terraria or aquaria are well suited for use as rain chambers. Tall thirty-gallon setups will suffice, but because larger rain chambers allow more space, we recommend them.

You can imitate rain in many different ways, but the best advice is to keep it simple. You can construct a water section by gluing a piece of glass to separate at least one-third of the setup. The glass need be only three or four inches high. Depending on how elaborate you want your setup to be, a hole drilled by the manufacturer in a piece of glass at the bottom of the water section will allow for drainage and a recirculating rain system. Alternatively, you can use a small powerhead-type pump in the water section of the rain chamber. Many pumps can be modified to fit garden misters, which create the "rain" that is necessary to induce this species to breed.

Red-eyed tree frogs in amplexus.

The use of an appliance timer allows for a regular rain schedule. Gravel or a similar substrate for the land section allows the frogs the land surface they need as the rain drenches the setup. Plants such as *Anthurium, Monstera, Philodendron,* and *Spathyphylum* are easily rooted in water and grow well in rain chambers. Avoid using potted plants because their soil will quickly spoil the water. Positioning leaves above the water will give searching females an ideal oviposition (egg-laying) site.

Condition your frogs with a high-nutrient feeding before making breeding attempts to assure your animals are in optimum health. If the frogs have been kept dry and the winter cold has past, you can most easily induce breeding in the spring months. If you align your breeding attempts with spring storms and decreases and increases in barometric pressure, you are likely to be rewarded with clutches of eggs. Raining from the late afternoon (five or six p.m.) into the late evening (eleven p.m. or twelve a.m.) yields the best results.

Amplexus (breeding/sexual embrace) usually occurs within the first couple of days, but sometimes it takes a couple of weeks. Feed the frogs continually, and take care to remove uneaten and dead crickets.

Remove all feces as soon as you see any. It is important to check the rain chamber frequently for eggs. Once you find clutches, you should remove them to containers in which the embryos can develop and the tadpoles can emerge. If clutches are oviposited on leaves, remove the entire leaf and hang it in the container a few inches above the water. If you find clutches on the glass, remove them and place them on leaves or other suitable sites above the water to incubate like the others.

The optimum temperature for egg incubation is between 74 and 78 degrees Fahrenheit (23–26 degrees Celsius). Constant temperatures below 70 degrees F (21 degrees C) and in excess of 80 degrees F (27 degrees C) may cause the developing embryos to die. It generally takes from six to nine days for the embryos to develop into tadpoles. When embryonic development is complete, the encapsulated tadpole wriggles its way free, sliding down the leaf into the water. A gentle mist will facilitate this emergence if the embryos have completely developed into tadpoles. Once eggs have hatched remove the tadpoles from their containers and place them in prepared rearing aquaria.

In order to avoid competition and overcrowding, divide your tadpoles into small groups. I use a series of ten-gallon aquariums containing three to five inches of water. Rearing containers may be plumbed together or kept separated.

Water quality, temperature, and feeding are the three most important factors in raising tadpoles into froglets. You should change the water in rearing setups every couple of days to avoid buildup of harmful chemicals, including ammonia and nitrates. If you use filtration, sponge filters available at aquarium stores work well. More advanced technology such as wet/dry filtration with frequent water changes has worked well for this author. Remember not to use tap water for your rearing aquaria. You must dechlorinate and dechloramine the water.

Keep the water temperature between 74 and 80 degrees F (23 and 27 degrees C). Lower temperatures will cause the tadpoles to develop more slowly, and higher temperatures can be fatal. You can keep the temperature constant with the use of a high-quality aquarium heater with a built-in thermostat.

Fish foods, such as Sera Micron® and flakes foods (which are easily pulverized), will work best for feeding your tadpoles. Feed them regularly, two to three times every day. Metamorphosis is usually completed in thirty to sixty days, although some stragglers may take longer.

When their front legs have emerged, your tadpoles will start to climb the side of the glass. At this point, remove the froglets and place them in setups that are similar to those of the adults, but keep these slightly more humid. Simple bare-bottom tanks with small potted plants work fine. Frequent misting will keep the vulnerable froglets from becoming too dry, but bear in mind that too much humidity at this stage leads to bloating (excessive absorption of water), which usually results in death. The key to success at this stage is careful observation, and adjustment if called for. Also make a small water dish available.

As the tadpoles are developing, it is wise to prepare small foods for the small froglets. You will need large amounts of pinhead to week-old crickets, fruit flies, and other small insects. The froglets will start to feed shortly after the few days it takes them to reabsorb their tails. Give young red-eyed tree frogs vitamin and calcium supplements with their food. Because young frogs grow at different rates and compete for food, it is suggested that you house them in small groups according to size. The froglets will grow relative to the amount of food allotted and frequency of feedings. As the growing tree frogs develop, you must make changes in diet and enclosure to accommodate them. Depending on their rate of growth, young frogs may become sexually mature in as little time as one year. But because of the inherent stresses, do not induce breeding until your animals are at least a year and a half old.

References

Duellman, W.E. *The Hylid Frogs of Middle America.* Museum of Natural History, University of Kansas, 1970.

Fenolio, D. and M.J. Ready. "Phyllomedusine Frogs of Latin America, in the Wild and in Captivity." *The Vivarium,* no. 5, 1994, pp. 26–29.

Savage, J.M. and J.R. Villa. *Herpetofauna of Costa Rica.* Society for the Study of Amphibians and Reptiles, 1988.

Our appreciation and thanks to Alan McCready and Michael Ready for their guidance and assistance with this chapter.

Part III
White's Tree Frogs and
White-lipped Tree Frogs

General Information

What's In a Name?

The current trend among herpetoculturists is to call amphibians and reptiles by their scientific names to avoid any confusion about the identification of the species to which one is referring. The scientific name of White's tree frog is *Litoria caerulea*. Frogs of the genus *Litoria* are members of the Pelodryadinae, a subfamily of the large family of tree frogs called the Hylidae. The species name *cuerule a* means "blue," a name that was presumably attributed to the color of preserved specimens. But most wild White's tree frogs are actually green, and occasional captive-bred White's metamorphose with a bluish skin that becomes more blue as they mature. Captive-raised "White's" maintained under low lighting also tend to lose the typical green coloration and become blue-green to blue.

Occasionally one will hear people call White's tree frogs, "white tree frogs." The name "White's tree frogs" refers to the name of the man who first described the species. In the pet trade, White's tree frogs are sold under a variety of names, usually White's tree frogs, dumpy tree frogs, Australian dumpy tree frogs, or, lately, Indonesian dumpy tree frogs to distinguish the latter from the forms originating from Australia.

Distribution

Northern and eastern Australia; islands in the Torres Straits; New Guinea and New Zealand (introduced)

Size

Large female White's tree frogs can reach a snout-to-vent length of four inches (10.2 cm) . Males are usually smaller.

Sexing

It can be difficult to reliably determine the sex of White's tree frogs, particularly in younger animals. The most reliable method is to keep them for a period of time and isolate males from a group as they begin calling (which they do by the age of one year). If isolation is not possible, then another method is to pick up individual adult frogs, placing your index and middle finger across the back and your thumb along the belly and chest area. Once a frog is firmly in hand, look on the inside of its thumbs. Males in varying degrees of breeding condition will have small brown "nuptial pads" on the inside of their "hands." If the frog is not in breeding condition, its nuptial pads will be so faint that they will be almost impossible to distinguish.

There are also other methods that can be used to determine the sexes. With males that are mature, slightly pressing with the thumb against its chest area will sometimes elicit a call or partial call. (Remember, we said slightly pressing; this means gentle pressure.) Another thing to do, but which is not very reliable, is to examine the skin of the throat just before the "fold" line across the chest. In males, the skin just before that line is often looser and slightly more gray than in females. Ultimately, calling and sexual behavior are the best indicators of sex.

Varieties of White's Tree Frogs

Herpetologists usually do not recognize varieties or forms of White's tree frogs based on characteristics that are selectively bred or associated with White's from different areas.

Two major distinctions are made by herpetoculturists, depending on area of origin. Thus, there are the original Australian White's and the more recently imported Indonesian White's. Most commercial breeders are making efforts to keep these varieties isolated.

Australian White's of the herpetocultural trade are characterized primarily by their bright green, blue green, or turquoise blue coloration. As a rule, the thick glandular supratympanic ridge in this variety is slight to moderate. Among breeders of Australian White's, selective breeding is in progress to produce highly white-spotted strains, a blue strain, and a pseudo-splendida strain that would combine large yellow-white spots on the back with the toad-like glands characteristic of *Litoria splendida* beneath the skin of the head.

Indonesian White's are often a dull green. The supratympanic ridge varies from slight to extreme, in which case fatty development can nearly cover their eyes. These Whites can vary in size from small (2 ° inches) to quite large. Females commonly develop greater glandular supratympanic ridges than males. Little selective breeding has been done with Indonesian White's but the large gene pool available as a result of the many thousands imported should offer future opportunities for the development of interesting new strains.

Longevity

There is a European record of a captive 21-year old White's tree frog still living at the time the age was reported. With a reasonable amount of care, captive-bred and raised animals can be expected to live ten years or more.

A pair of White's tree frogs in amplexus.

Housing and General Maintenance

WHITE'S TREE FROGS are best housed in tall, all-glass vivaria with screen tops. Juveniles of these frogs can be housed in vivaria as small as a standard 5- or 5 1/2- gallon vivarium or 10-gallon vivarium but will require a larger enclosure within a year. Minimum enclosure size for adult White's tree frogs should be a standard 20-gallon high vivarium with a standard 29-gallon being even more desirable. Standard 10-gallon vivaria are not tall enough for adequate display of adults and seriously limit their natural level of activity. On the other hand, the custom 18-gallon high vivaria with screen tops sold by some companies are ideal for small numbers of this species. For display of larger numbers or for purely aesthetic purposes, larger and taller vivaria are recommended.

If you are using a large vivarium, 40 gallons or more, to house a group of White's tree frogs, one option is to create a water area by attaching a pre-cut piece of glass to the bottom and sides of the enclosure with silicone adhesive. Maintenance of this water area requires regular cleaning and siphoning. In a very large vivarium (60 gallons or more), you can use a water pump to create a miniature waterfall. The use of a water pump will also allow you to run the water through a filtering medium (which can be as simple as filter pads or aquarium filter floss), as well as to facilitate cleaning and siphoning.

Ground Media

From a purely practical point of view, newspaper, plain newsprint, or brown paper (similar to that of grocery bags) can be used as a ground medium for White's tree frogs. This is the medium recommended for dealers or stores who must house large numbers of these frogs. Such media are inexpensive and allow for regular and easy replacement, thus reducing possible outbreaks of disease as a result of bacterial

An outdoor screen enclosure with live plants for raising baby White's tree frogs.

growth or toxins from wastes that could be reabsorbed through the frogs's skin.

For display purposes, there are two possible ground media. One, recommended only for use in larger vivaria (29 gallons or more), consists of using a 2 inch layer of a peat-based potting soil (one that does not contain perlite for drainage or added fertilizers) over a layer of drainage consisting of 1 inch to 1 1/2 inches of pea gravel or coarse aquarium gravel. This mixture will allow you to create a planted vivarium if you desire.

The other option is to use 1 inch to 1 1/2 inches of medium-grade orchid bark at the bottom of the vivarium. Vivaria with orchid bark can be decorated by using selected pieces of wood, rocks, and potted plants concealed by vivarium landscape elements.

Some people also use orchid bark as a top layer over ground media for decorative purposes and to reduce surface moisture of the ground medium. The bark should be kept dry and care should be given to obtain fir-based bark, never cedar.

Screen Covers

The vivaria of White's tree frogs should have tightly fitting screen covers, preferably with a locking mechanism. Do not use a solid glass cover or a cover with just a few ventilation holes. White's tree frogs require good ventilation in order to thrive, and at least 50 percent of the cover should allow for free air flow. A poorly designed cover can lead to escape and the eventual discovery of a dust-covered, dried out, White's tree frog "mummy."

Landscaping the Vivarium

In larger vivaria with potting soil as a primary ground medium, the following elements can be used to create an attractive vivarium. Used toward the back of the vivarium, slabs of cork bark provide an interesting background as well as vertical shelters and climbing areas for White's. Cork bark can often be obtained from pet stores that specialize in reptiles. As background plants to be planted in front of the cork bark, the best are broad-leafed snakeplants (*Sansevieria*). Often you can find these in the houseplant sections of supermarkets, and they are almost always available from nurseries specializing in houseplants. The most readily available are the variegated *S. trifasciata* and *S. "Moonshine,"* a very attractive, pale green, broad-leafed cultivar. Sansevierias are tough plants, capable of surviving the abuse of active White's tree frogs. They need moderate to strong light and moderate watering. A soggy soil will cause the roots and eventually the entire plant to rot, so keep this in mind when you water the ground medium.

In the foreground, freshwater driftwood or small curled pieces of cork bark can be added as climbing areas for White's. One or two pieces placed diagonally inside the vivarium are usually sufficient. White's tree frogs need room to move so creating any kind of tangle is undesirable.

White's tree frogs do everything with vigor, and that includes moving about the vivarium. This makes selecting foreground plants for their vivaria a difficult task. Whites will usually end up crushing any thin-leafed or soft-stemmed species you introduce into the vivarium. In very large vivaria, the cut-leaf philodendron, *Monstera deliciosa*, will usually manage to survive because its thick stems will withstand any permanent damage and its broad leaves will either support a Whites or cause it to drop. In smaller vivaria, the best you can do is resign yourself to having no foreground plants for decorative purposes except low plants or ground covers. Good choices for this purpose are the bird's nest sansevieria, *S.t.* "Hahnii" and some of the spineless bromeliads such as neoregelias.

In vivaria using only orchid bark as a ground medium, all of the forementioned plants can be used but the plants should be introduced in plastic pots, partially buried in the ground medium, and concealed and held in place by landscape structures.

Water

White's tree frogs should have clean water available at all times. Thus, you should introduce water either in a large porcelain bowl or a glass dish— or, if you have a built-in water area, in the water section of your vivarium. The water depth should be no higher than the height of your White's tree frogs (legs folded) when at rest. With juveniles, place a small rock in the water bowl to allow the frogs to climb in and out easily. It is not uncommon for juvenile White's tree frogs to drown in water bowls or dishes whose water is too deep and sides are too steep for the frog to climb out. So remember, THINK TREE FROG.

People in some areas of the United States appear to have difficulty in keeping White's tree frogs alive, even though this is a very easy species to maintain. If you have problems with this species, it is a good idea to consider water quality as a possible cause. For maintaining juveniles it is a good idea to dechlorinate the water by using the standard dechlorinators sold in the fish trade. If you have any doubts about the quality of your tap water, use bottled drinking water, but definitely not distilled water. Whites do best in water that is slightly alkaline and moderately hard.

Temperature

White's tree frogs should be maintained at temperatures of 76° to 85° F. They can safely tolerate temperature drops at night to 65° F. You can use several methods to heat a White's tree frog vivarium. During the day, you can place low-wattage incandescent bulbs over select basking areas, usually part of a branch or slab of bark, so that the highest temperature of the area nearest to the light is 85° F.

Other methods preferred by most herpetoculturists consist of using heat cables on a rheostat, heat strips, or heating pads beneath the vivarium. Others use submersible heaters in a water area or in jars. "Hot rocks" are not suitable for White's tree frogs because their surface temperature is too high. At night, if you have no other heat source available, you can use a low-wattage red incandescent bulb as a heat source.

Whatever heating system you use, calibrate the temperature carefully so that it is within the range desirable for the welfare of your White's tree frogs. Also, carefully read instructions regarding the use of any heating system, in order to prevent risks of electrocution or fires.

Other Lighting

For maintaining plants and for lighting your White's tree frog vivarium, full-spectrum fluorescent bulbs such as VitaLite® are recommended. They allow your plants to flourish and bring out natural colors, both in animals and in plants. In a smaller vivarium, at least one fluorescent bulb running its length is recommended; for larger ones, two or more. With low lights, plants will etiolate (grow pale and thin) and eventually be crushed by frogs and die.

If you cannot afford fluorescent lighting, don't worry; White's can be maintained in a plantless vivarium, receiving only bright indirect light from a window. Just make sure that you never place your vivarium in direct sunlight, which can result in a cooked White's during a bright summer day.

Maintaining the Vivarium

As you will soon discover, any frog with the *joie de vivre* of a White's tree frog can make a mess of a vivarium in no time at all. White's eat large amounts of food and consequently defecate copiously, usually but not always in the water area, which therefore needs regular cleaning and replacement. White's also may defecate on various select areas in the vivarium, such as plants and wood. In a large vivarium, daily misting in the early evening can help keep most of these areas clean. Another habit that White's tree frogs have is to smear varying amounts of their skin mucus on the sides of the glass. Regular misting can help keep the glass of their enclosure clean.

Despite regular mistings, there will come a time, every couple of weeks or so, when it is necessary to spray the sides of the vivarium with water and use a plastic scrub pad or single-edged razor to rub off the thin coat of mucus. Finishing up with a moist paper towel will restore the viewing clarity of the glass.

Feeding White's Tree Frogs

PROPER FEEDING AND vitamin/mineral supplementation is critical for the long-term survival of White's tree frogs. As juveniles, White's tree frogs have high calcium requirements to meet the demands of their rapidly growing skeletal system. With insufficient calcium, froglets die or, when treated too late, develop into adults with varying degrees of skeletal deformities.

Recommended foods for White's tree frogs are as follows:

For juveniles (1/2 inch to 1 1/2 inches): Offer food daily by placing near your froglets crickets that are two to three weeks old (they should be no longer than the length of a froglet's head). Twice a week coat with a reptile multivitamin supplement and calcium carbonate (1 part supplement to 3 parts calcium).

How juveniles are fed is important. If froglets do not consume the crickets soon after they are introduced, most of the supplements on the crickets will come off and you may end up with froglets that develop calcium deficiencies. Thus it is better to feed White's at night, when they are more likely to be active, than during the daytime, when they are usually asleep in corners of vertical shelters.

For subadults to adults (1 1/2 to 3 inches): Every two to three days, feed 3 to 4-week-old crickets coated as previously mentioned once a week. If your frogs will take them, you can also offer a one- or two-day-old "pink" mouse every two to four weeks. You can dip the mouse's rump in calcium if you think your frog may not be getting enough calcium from the crickets.

Adults: Two to three times per week, feed adult frogs large crickets and occasional early-stage "fuzzy" mice.

To prevent problems associated with excessive calcium intake, supplement crickets and other insects at only one feeding per week.

If you want your White's to live a long time, monitor their diets and do not allow them to become obese. Fat White's may look cute and dumpy or bizarre because of extensive supratympanic glandular development, but these excessive fat reserves can also make them more prone to disease and can shorten their life spans.

Breeding

IF PROPERLY MAINTAINED, captive-raised Australian White's tree frogs will reach sexual maturity in their second year. For breeding purposes, select only healthy adult pairs with good weight. You should precondition them for breeding during the cool months (ideally, late winter) by placing them in a clean, partially covered, sterile vivarium in a cool area of your facility so that they are exposed to temperatures of 65 degrees for as many as 16 hours per day. Keep the vivarium in the dark and provide vertical shelters.Offer no food during this time.

You should cool your White's tree frogs under the above schedule for six weeks prior to attempting to breed them. Following the cooling period, maintain them under optimal conditions with adequate heat, and feed them regularly for two to four weeks.

The next step is to induce breeding. You can do this by placing White's tree frogs in a large aquarium or an other large enclosure with 3 to 4 inches of aged quality water to which you have added water plants such as *Anachris* or water hyacinth and floating foam platforms. Using a water pump, construct a rain chamber by running water through a large plastic container with multiple holes drilled in it, or through drilled PVC pipe with a cappped end. Make sure that a screen covers the top of the vivarium to prevent escape. Introduce the frogs and set the rain chamber on a timer so that it "rains" from six p.m. to ten p.m. Breeding will usually occur after two to five days of this schedule during the "off phase" of the rain chamber. Several thousand eggs are usually laid. After breeding occurs, remove the parents, turn off the rain chamber, and add an airstone (connected to an air pump) in the water. Hatching, at a temperature of 80 to 85° F, will begin in 28 to 36 hours. Following hatching, tadpoles will go into an inactive stage in which they rest on the bottom, but within 24 to 36 hours they will cling to the sides of the vivarium and plants.

Rearing the tadpoles will require you to use several hundred gallons of aged quality water (dechlorinated, dechloramined, and aged enough to allow for dissipation of most water-dissolved gasses) maintained at a temperature of 80 to 85 degrees F. The tanks should receive either natural sunlight (if in a greenhouse or in a warm area), or light from full-spectrum fluorescent lights. Make sure that there are live plants in the water. As a general rule, better success is obtained with White's raised in large pools with live plants and natural light than under sterile laboratory conditions.

Starting with the fourth day after hatching, you can feed the tadpoles a high-quality tropical fish flake food twice per day. Keeping the water reasonably clean is important during the rearing stage as is keeping the tadpoles in uncrowded conditions (a maximum of 15 tadpoles per gallon of water). You must be careful to maintain the quality of the water. Make sure that it is dechlorinated, dechloraminated and aged.

The first metamorphosing frogs will emerge during the fourth week, and metamorphosis will extend for several weeks. Be sure to provide plants or platforms that allow the emerging froglets to climb out of the water or they will drown. The biggest challenge of breeding White's is providing housing and maintenance for hundreds or thousands of froglets. Under overcrowded conditions, the froglet mortality rate will be very high. Ideally, you will provide large screen enclosures or screen houses, which are the best housing for large numbers of froglets.

The next challenge is feeding hundreds or thousands of froglets with high food requirements. It can be expensive as well as time consuming. For private breeders who wish simply to raise a small number of White's for themselves or for trade or sale, the wisest thing to do is to limit, at the tadpole stage, the number of froglets that you can accommodate. Houseflies are an inexpensive dietary component for raising large numbers of froglets.

White-lipped Tree Frogs

U NTIL THE RECENT glut of imported Indonesian white-lipped tree frogs, this species used to be another of the tree frogs that herpetoculturists used to dream of being able to own.

In its own right, the white-lipped tree frog is a large and beautiful tree frog that like the White's tree frog, can be displayed in attractive vivaria. Compared to White's, this is a restless species that cannot readily be handled and that will secrete a sticky whitish mucus if handled excessively. Always wash your hands after handling them. They are also more delicate and less cold tolerant that White's tree frogs.

What's in a Name?

The scientific name of the white-lipped tree frog is *Litoria infrafrenata*. They are usually sold under the name of white-lipped tree frog's, but some dealers sell them as Indonesian giant green tree frogs.

Varieties of White-lipped Tree Frogs

All white-lipped tree frogs are not alike. The most attractive are the large forms from Australia, which have a finely textured skin and are bright green with orange immediately behind their arms. The white-lipped tree frogs currently being imported in large numbers from Indonesia can vary a great deal. The most attractive are bright green with broad pearl-white margins along their hindlegs, while the least attractive are a dull dark green. In captivity, many white-lipped tree frogs become faded green or blue-green. Some of the Indonesian frogs can become a dirty green. The cause of this color loss may be the quality of lighting (those raised in greenhouses are often a brighter green, as are White's tree frogs) or a dietary deficiency.

Distribution: Cape York Peninsula, Queensland, Australia, and New Guinea; New Ireland, Bismarck Archipelago; introduced into Java.

Size: As big as five inches (12.7 cm) for large females. Males are smaller.

Sexing: Males are smaller than females. The throat of males is darker than that of females and has looser skin. Mature males ready to breed have dark nuptial pads on the inside of their "thumbs."

General care and maintenance: White-lipped tree frogs can be maintained in a manner similiar to White's tree frogs, except that they are less tolerant of cold. They also require higher relative humidity, which can be provided by covering up to 50 percent of the vivarium enclosure and by giving them a light misting early each evening.

Longevity: The authors have kept white-lipped tree frogs, obtained as adults, for six years, and they were still alive at the time they were sold. Potential longevity is probably at least ten years.

Breeding: Similiar to White's tree frogs except that night temperatures should be dropped only to between 70 and 74 degrees F. Froglets of *L. infrafrenata* are generally more delicate and more difficult to raise the White's froglets. Calcium deficiency and varying degrees of skeletal deformity are common to captive-raised white-lipped tree frogs because of inadequate feeding procedures.

Source Material

Cogger. M.G., 1975. "Reptiles and Amphibians of Australia." Ralph Curtis Books, pp. 84–91.

de Vosjoli, P., and R. Mailloux, 1987. "Methods and Problems of the Large Scale Propagation of Tropical Frogs." Proceedings of the Eleventh International Symposium on Captive Propagation and Husbandry, pp. 25–34.

Duellman, W.E., and L. Truebb, 1986. "Biology of the Amphibians." McGraw Hill.

Frost, D. (ed), 1985. "Amphibian Species of the World." Lawrence, Kansas, Assoc. Syst. Coll.

McClain, J.M., and R. A. Odum, and T.C. Shely, 1983. "Hormonally Induced Breeding and Rearing of White's Tree frogs *(Litoria caerulea)*." Proceedings of the Seventh Annual Reptile Symposium on Captive Propagation and Husbandry, pp. 34–39.

Useful Sources of Information

The American Federation of Herpetoculturists (AFH) offers its members a bi-monthly, full-color journal dedicated to the dissemination of information on reptiles and amphibians. Write to: PO Box 300067, Escondido, CA 92030. Tel# (619) 747-4948.

The International Hylid Society, 2607 Thomas Rd., Valparaiso, IN 46383.

Drew Ready can be reached at:
Internet Address: drew_ready@otter.monterey.edu

Amphibian Medicine

Wright K. 1996. "Amphibian Husbandry and Medicine," in *Reptile Medicine and Surgery*, edited by D. Mader, W.B. Saunders Company.

Index